★★★★★★★★★★★ HARCOURT HORIZONS

People and Communities

Activity Book

Harcourt

Orlando   Austin   Chicago   New York   Toronto   London   San Diego

Visit *The Learning Site!*
www.harcourtschool.com

Printed in the United States of America

ISBN 0-15-322596-3

2 3 4 5 6 7 8 9 10 073 10 09 08 07 06 05 04 03 02

The activities in this book reinforce social studies concepts and skills in **Harcourt Horizons: People and Communities.** There is one activity for every lesson and skill in the Pupil Edition. Copies of the activity pages appear with answers in the Teacher's Edition. In addition to activities, this book also contains reproductions of the graphic organizers that appear in the Chapter Reviews in the Pupil Edition. Multiple-choice test preparation pages for student practice are also provided. A blank multiple-choice answer sheet can be found after these content pages.

Contents

Name _____ Date _____

Multiple-Choice
Answer Sheet

Number your answers to match the questions on the test preparation page.

____	Ⓐ	Ⓑ	Ⓒ	Ⓓ		____	Ⓐ	Ⓑ	Ⓒ	Ⓓ		____	Ⓐ	Ⓑ	Ⓒ	Ⓓ
____	Ⓕ	Ⓖ	Ⓗ	Ⓙ		____	Ⓕ	Ⓖ	Ⓗ	Ⓙ		____	Ⓕ	Ⓖ	Ⓗ	Ⓙ
____	Ⓐ	Ⓑ	Ⓒ	Ⓓ		____	Ⓐ	Ⓑ	Ⓒ	Ⓓ		____	Ⓐ	Ⓑ	Ⓒ	Ⓓ
____	Ⓕ	Ⓖ	Ⓗ	Ⓙ		____	Ⓕ	Ⓖ	Ⓗ	Ⓙ		____	Ⓕ	Ⓖ	Ⓗ	Ⓙ
____	Ⓐ	Ⓑ	Ⓒ	Ⓓ		____	Ⓐ	Ⓑ	Ⓒ	Ⓓ		____	Ⓐ	Ⓑ	Ⓒ	Ⓓ

____	Ⓐ	Ⓑ	Ⓒ	Ⓓ		____	Ⓐ	Ⓑ	Ⓒ	Ⓓ		____	Ⓐ	Ⓑ	Ⓒ	Ⓓ
____	Ⓕ	Ⓖ	Ⓗ	Ⓙ		____	Ⓕ	Ⓖ	Ⓗ	Ⓙ		____	Ⓕ	Ⓖ	Ⓗ	Ⓙ
____	Ⓐ	Ⓑ	Ⓒ	Ⓓ		____	Ⓐ	Ⓑ	Ⓒ	Ⓓ		____	Ⓐ	Ⓑ	Ⓒ	Ⓓ
____	Ⓕ	Ⓖ	Ⓗ	Ⓙ		____	Ⓕ	Ⓖ	Ⓗ	Ⓙ		____	Ⓕ	Ⓖ	Ⓗ	Ⓙ
____	Ⓐ	Ⓑ	Ⓒ	Ⓓ		____	Ⓐ	Ⓑ	Ⓒ	Ⓓ		____	Ⓐ	Ⓑ	Ⓒ	Ⓓ

____	Ⓐ	Ⓑ	Ⓒ	Ⓓ		____	Ⓐ	Ⓑ	Ⓒ	Ⓓ		____	Ⓐ	Ⓑ	Ⓒ	Ⓓ
____	Ⓕ	Ⓖ	Ⓗ	Ⓙ		____	Ⓕ	Ⓖ	Ⓗ	Ⓙ		____	Ⓕ	Ⓖ	Ⓗ	Ⓙ
____	Ⓐ	Ⓑ	Ⓒ	Ⓓ		____	Ⓐ	Ⓑ	Ⓒ	Ⓓ		____	Ⓐ	Ⓑ	Ⓒ	Ⓓ
____	Ⓕ	Ⓖ	Ⓗ	Ⓙ		____	Ⓕ	Ⓖ	Ⓗ	Ⓙ		____	Ⓕ	Ⓖ	Ⓗ	Ⓙ
____	Ⓐ	Ⓑ	Ⓒ	Ⓓ		____	Ⓐ	Ⓑ	Ⓒ	Ⓓ		____	Ⓐ	Ⓑ	Ⓒ	Ⓓ

____	Ⓐ	Ⓑ	Ⓒ	Ⓓ		____	Ⓐ	Ⓑ	Ⓒ	Ⓓ		____	Ⓐ	Ⓑ	Ⓒ	Ⓓ
____	Ⓕ	Ⓖ	Ⓗ	Ⓙ		____	Ⓕ	Ⓖ	Ⓗ	Ⓙ		____	Ⓕ	Ⓖ	Ⓗ	Ⓙ
____	Ⓐ	Ⓑ	Ⓒ	Ⓓ		____	Ⓐ	Ⓑ	Ⓒ	Ⓓ		____	Ⓐ	Ⓑ	Ⓒ	Ⓓ
____	Ⓕ	Ⓖ	Ⓗ	Ⓙ		____	Ⓕ	Ⓖ	Ⓗ	Ⓙ		____	Ⓕ	Ⓖ	Ⓗ	Ⓙ
____	Ⓐ	Ⓑ	Ⓒ	Ⓓ		____	Ⓐ	Ⓑ	Ⓒ	Ⓓ		____	Ⓐ	Ⓑ	Ⓒ	Ⓓ

My Community

Directions How much do you know about your community? Complete the sentence or circle the answer. If you need more ideas, ask your family and friends.

1 Where I Live

The name of my community is _____.

My community is: small   medium   large

2 Businesses

Many people buy groceries at _____.

Some people buy clothing at _____.

3 What We Do to Have Fun

My favorite place to play is _____.

I like to visit _____.

Directions Draw a picture of your favorite place in your community.

Organize It

Directions Use this graphic organizer to help you summarize the main idea of the lesson. Read the main idea of the lesson in the center. Write details on the blank lines. List skills people have. List service and safety jobs.

People have different skills.

_____

_____

_____

Main Idea

People in a community have different jobs and depend on one another.

A community depends on many people.

_____

_____

_____

Use after reading Chapter 1, Lesson 2, pages 16–19.

© Harcourt

Name _____ Date _____

CHART AND GRAPH SKILLS
Read Graphs

Directions Look at the picture graph and answer the questions below. Then complete the bar graph to show the same information.

Picture Graph of Hospitals in Six States

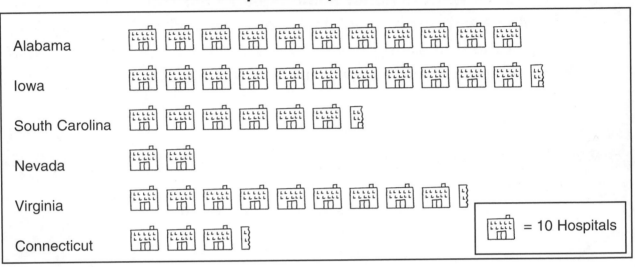

1 How many hospitals are there in South Carolina? _____

2 Which state has the most hospitals? _____

3 Which has fewer hospitals, Alabama or Iowa? _____

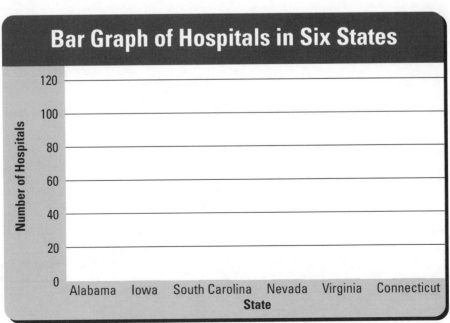

© Harcourt

Celebrate!

Directions Create your own holiday and celebration. You might want to honor someone special. You might want to celebrate a special time of year, such as the day of the first spring flower. Once you have chosen your holiday, decide how you will celebrate.

Reason for the Holiday _____

_____

Day of the Year You Will Hold the Celebration _____

_____

Special Activities During the Celebration _____

_____

_____

Directions Draw a symbol to represent your holiday.

Making Laws

Directions You may have ideas for laws that would make life better in your community. Think about the laws you would write. Then fill in the blanks below.

Law #1: _____

_____

Why This Law Is Needed: _____

_____

_____

What the Consequences Should Be for Breaking This Law: ____

_____

Law #2: _____

_____

Why This Law Is Needed: _____

_____

What the Consequences Should Be for Breaking This Law: ____

_____

Name _____ Date _____

READING SKILLS
Solve a Problem

Directions Read about the problem that two students are having. Then fill in the blanks.

     Darren and Rose both want to use the same climbing equipment at recess. Rose's friend Alice says that Darren used the equipment all last recess and no one else got to use it. Darren says that Rose was on it all the previous day. Ms. Seth, the playground teacher, says everyone must share the equipment.

Identify the problem. _____

_____

What do you know about the problem? _____

_____

_____

List possible solutions and their consequences.

Possible Solution	Possible Consequence

Choose the best solution.

Why do you think your solution will work? _____

        Use after reading Chapter 1, Skill Lesson, pages 30–31.

© Harcourt

Why People Live in Communities

Directions Complete the graphic organizer to show that you understand the main idea and details of each lesson.

MAIN IDEAS	SUPPORTING DETAILS
People live in communities for many reasons.	_____ _____ _____
_____ _____ _____	People have different skills. People depend on one another for safety.
People with the same interests form groups.	_____ _____ _____ _____
_____ _____ _____	Laws keep people safe. The mayor leads the community government.

Use after reading Chapter 1, pages 10–33.

Name _____ Date _____

Test Preparation

Directions Read each question and choose the best answer. Then fill in the circle for the answer you have chosen. Be sure to fill in the circle completely.

1 Walt Disney is best known as a—
- Ⓐ writer of poetry.
- Ⓑ builder of EPCOT and other theme parks.
- Ⓒ teacher of science.
- Ⓓ inventor of telephones.

2 Needs are—
- Ⓕ work that someone does.
- Ⓖ materials from nature.
- Ⓗ things we all must have.
- Ⓙ places where people can learn.

3 "Flight Days" celebrates the time when young bald eagles—
- Ⓐ build their own nests.
- Ⓑ learn how to fly with other eagles.
- Ⓒ gather food.
- Ⓓ get their flight feathers.

4 What happens because of what a person does is called a—
- Ⓕ responsibility.
- Ⓖ consequence.
- Ⓗ law.
- Ⓙ custom.

5 The job of a mayor is to—
- Ⓐ make laws for the community.
- Ⓑ decide whether a person has broken the law.
- Ⓒ see that the community's problems are solved.
- Ⓓ remember important events.

© Harcourt

Use after reading Chapter 1, pages 10–33.

Mapping the World

Directions Write the name of each continent on the line below the shape. Look at the maps in your textbook if you need help.

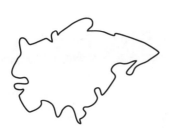

_____

_____

_____

_____

_____

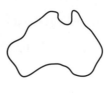

_____

_____

© Harcourt

MAP AND GLOBE SKILLS
Read a Map

Directions Look at the map of Galveston, Texas. Use your map skills to answer the questions.

1 In which direction would you travel if you landed at the airport and needed to go to

Galveston Bay? _____

2 What does the symbol ⍟

stand for? _____

3 What body of water is Seawall

Boulevard next to? _____

_____

4 If you traveled all the way along Anderson Way Road, about how far would you go in miles? About how far would you go in kilometers?

_____

_____

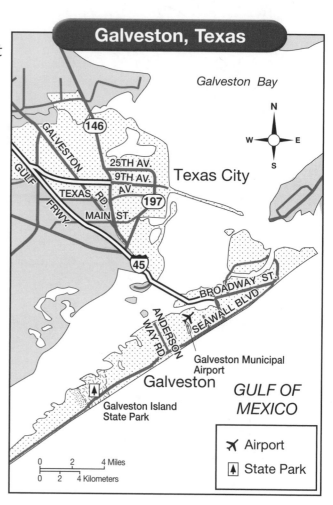

5 Which body of water is farther north, Galveston Bay or the Gulf of

Mexico? _____

Use after reading Chapter 2, Skill Lesson, pages 42–43.

Name _____   Date _____

Name That Term

Directions Write the vocabulary word that best fits each description.

| rural | suburb | capital city | population | President | transportation |

A city's is large. A small town's is small. It tells how many live in each place.

_____

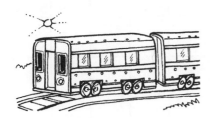

Many people in suburbs and cities use buses and trains to get to work. It is a way of moving people from one place to another.

_____

We only have one of these leaders at a time. This person leads our national government.

_____

If you live on a farm, you live in this type of community.

_____

Washington, D.C., is this for the United States. If you are a lawmaker for our country, you go here to make laws.

_____

If you live here, you do not live in a city, but you live very near one.

_____

A Puzzling Community

Directions For each question, find the box with the same number. Fill in the boxes under each number with the word that best completes the sentence. When you have finished, read across the bold line of letters and answer this question:

What was found in the mountains near Eagle in the 1880s?

1 Your great-grandmother is your _____.

2 A person who helps settle a new land is called a _____.

3 William Edwards started the _____ that later became Eagle.

4 Eagle is not only the name of the town, but also the name of the _____.

5 C.F. Nogal was the _____ of, or the person who started, the first businesses in Eagle.

6 The story of what happened in a place is its _____.

Use after reading Chapter 2, Lesson 3, pages 48–53.

Name _____   Date _____

CHART AND GRAPH SKILLS
Using a Time Line

Directions Use the time line to answer the questions.

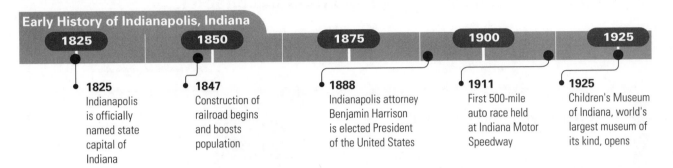

Early History of Indianapolis, Indiana

| 1825 | 1850 | 1875 | 1900 | 1925 |

1825
Indianapolis is officially named state capital of Indiana

1847
Construction of railroad begins and boosts population

1888
Indianapolis attorney Benjamin Harrison is elected President of the United States

1911
First 500-mile auto race held at Indiana Motor Speedway

1925
Children's Museum of Indiana, world's largest museum of its kind, opens

1 How many years are covered by the time line? _____

_____

2 Which happened first, the construction of the railroad or the first

500-mile auto race? _____

3 What took place in 1925? _____

4 In what year was Benjamin Harrison elected President? _____

5 How many years passed between the beginning of the construction of

the railroad and the first 500-mile auto race? _____

Location and History of Communities

Directions Complete the graphic organizer to show the clues and the conclusions you reached as you read the chapter.

CLUES	CONCLUSIONS

1. It helps you find your state.

2. You can see the four oceans on it.

3. It shows you the North and South Poles.

_____
_____
_____
_____

1. _____

2. _____

3. _____

The community of Eagle, Colorado, has changed over time.

Use after reading Chapter 2, pages 34–59.

© Harcourt

Name _____ Date _____

Test Preparation

Directions Read each question and choose the best answer. Then fill in the circle for the answer you have chosen. Be sure to fill in the circle completely.

1 A globe shows the true shapes of the oceans and continents because it—

 Ⓐ can be divided in half.

 Ⓑ can show what continents people live on.

 Ⓒ is round like the Earth.

 Ⓓ is a picture that shows the location of things.

2 Every place on Earth is in at least—

 Ⓕ one hemisphere.

 Ⓖ two hemispheres.

 Ⓗ three hemispheres.

 Ⓙ four hemispheres.

3 *North, south, east,* and *west* are—

 Ⓐ found on a map key.

 Ⓑ cardinal directions.

 Ⓒ the only directions you can follow.

 Ⓓ used to measure how far it is between two places on a map.

4 Washington, D.C., is an important city because—

 Ⓕ it is the capital city of the United States.

 Ⓖ it is a suburb.

 Ⓗ George Washington lived there.

 Ⓙ it has a good public transportation system.

5 Ancestors are—

 Ⓐ the first people to settle in a place.

 Ⓑ people who start settlements.

 Ⓒ people in a person's family who lived a long time ago.

 Ⓓ people who live in rural areas.

Use after reading Chapter 2, pages 34–59.

Volunteers Needed!

Directions Read about 12 citizens who want to volunteer. Then read the four ads. Organize the citizens into the groups in which you think they can best serve the community. Write their names under the ads.

- Mr. Johnson owns the lumberyard.
- Nancy Lane is a pet groomer.
- Jennifer Smith enjoys baking.
- Ms. Harris teaches tap dancing.
- Shannon McMahon is a pet sitter.
- Hank Ross is a housepainter.
- Mrs. Lee is a retired chef.

- Don Miles plays the clarinet.
- Sam Hill has a van.
- Brenda Jackson is an electrician.
- Sandra Mason is a piano teacher.
- Mrs. Lewis can volunteer on the weekends.

Volunteers Needed!
Help repair homes
damaged by flood!

Volunteer Performers Needed!
Contact the
entertainment committee for
the Annual Community Concert.

Help!
We need volunteer dog walkers
at Haven Animal Shelter
afternoons and weekends.

Volunteers Needed!
Lunch on Wheels
Help prepare or deliver meals.

Use after reading Chapter 3, Lesson 1, pages 74–77.

Name _____   Date _____

Law and Order

(Directions) **Find and circle the situations that show people who are not obeying community rules or laws. Then list the rules or laws that should be obeyed.**

1 _____   5 _____

2 _____   6 _____

3 _____   7 _____

4 _____   8 _____

CITIZENSHIP SKILLS
Resolve Conflict

Directions Study the scene. What might the conflict be about? Write what you think the two students are saying to each other. Then continue their conversation, or write a story to tell how they resolve the conflict.

_____

_____

_____

_____

_____

Use after reading Chapter 3, Skill Lesson, pages 82–83.

© Harcourt

Important Services

Directions Find and circle the words in the puzzle to complete the sentences below. Look across, down, and diagonally.

R	T	E	R	A	M	A	W	T	R	E
D	E	P	A	R	T	M	E	N	T	S
L	D	C	I	T	I	Z	E	N	S	E
I	U	P	R	O	P	E	R	T	Y	R
B	C	U	H	E	P	S	G	X	M	V
R	A	A	E	R	A	A	A	O	Y	I
A	T	L	P	Y	A	T	R	L	L	C
R	I	E	L	X	O	L	I	K	E	E
I	O	C	R	Y	Z	B	T	O	R	S
E	N	W	T	H	K	S	S	H	N	X
S	C	M	P	M	I	R	B	T	Y	A
P	U	B	L	I	C	W	O	R	K	S

Community governments provide many important _____.

The police, fire, and health _____ help _____

stay safe and healthy. The board of _____ makes decisions
about the community's schools. Communities also provide resources for fun

and _____ and _____ for lifelong learning.

The _____ department sees to everyday needs such as
garbage collection and road repairs. The government collects

_____ and _____ taxes to pay for all the
services, public buildings, and equipment.

Government Charts

Directions Write the name of each branch of the government in the first chart. Choose the correct representative for each branch from the box. Then do the same for the levels of government in the second chart. Representatives can be used more than once if needed.

Representatives

President	Mayor
Governor	Member of Board of Supervisors
Supreme Court Justice	Senator

Branches of the National Government

	Branch	Representative
1.	_____	_____
2.	_____	_____
3.	_____	_____

Levels of Government

	Level	Representative
1.	_____	_____
2.	_____	_____
3.	_____	_____
		_____
		_____
4.	_____	_____
		_____

© Harcourt

Name _____   Date _____

MAP AND GLOBE SKILLS

Identify State Capitals and Borders

Directions Label the states on the map that border North Carolina. Then use the map to answer the questions.

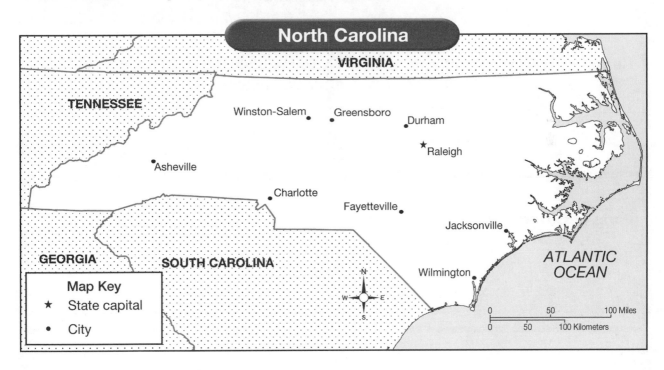

North Carolina

VIRGINIA

TENNESSEE

Winston-Salem · · Greensboro

·Durham

★Raleigh

·Asheville

·Charlotte

Fayetteville·

Jacksonville·

GEORGIA   SOUTH CAROLINA

Wilmington·

ATLANTIC OCEAN

Map Key
★ State capital
· City

0   50   100 Miles
0   50   100 Kilometers

1 What is the state capital of North Carolina? _____

2 What are the names of the states that border North Carolina?

_____

3 Is Winston-Salem east or west of Greensboro?

_____

4 Is Wilmington or Fayetteville closer to the Atlantic Ocean?

_____

© Harcourt

Parts of and Reasons for Government

Directions Complete the graphic organizer to show that you understand how to categorize information from the chapter.

CATEGORY	INFORMATION
Reasons for Government	To maintain order and security in our country
Parts of Government	_____ _____ _____
_____ _____ _____	national state local
People in Government	_____ _____ _____

Use after reading Chapter 3, pages 72–99.

3

Name _____   Date _____

Test Preparation

Directions Read each question and choose the best answer. Then fill in the circle for the answer you have chosen. Be sure to fill in the circle completely.

1 Public service is doing work—
- Ⓐ for money.
- Ⓑ for the good of the community.
- Ⓒ only in large cities.
- Ⓓ only during times of trouble.

2 Private property is property that—
- Ⓕ includes parks, streets, and roads.
- Ⓖ belongs to everyone in the community.
- Ⓗ belongs to one person or to a group of people.
- Ⓙ can be used by anyone for recreation.

3 Work done by the government for everyone in a city or town is known as—
- Ⓐ volunteering.
- Ⓑ recreation.
- Ⓒ a government service.
- Ⓓ a continuing education.

4 The public works department—
- Ⓕ cares for community swimming pools.
- Ⓖ helps people continue their education.
- Ⓗ offers special programs for children.
- Ⓙ collects garbage and keeps streets clean and in good repair.

5 The executive branch of government is responsible for—
- Ⓐ seeing that laws are obeyed.
- Ⓑ making laws.
- Ⓒ deciding whether laws are fair.
- Ⓓ rewriting laws.

Our National Government

Directions Answer the questions below to show what you have learned about our national government.

1 Fill in the following chart.

Branch of Government	What It Does

2 The state of Wyoming is larger than the state of Massachusetts. However, the state of Wyoming sends fewer representatives to Congress. Explain.

_____

_____

3 How many senators represent each state? _____

4 Describe three duties of the President of the United States.

_____

_____

_____

5 Why is the Supreme Court the most important court in the land?

_____

_____

Use after reading Chapter 4, Lesson 1, pages 102–107.

Name _____ Date _____

CHART AND GRAPH SKILLS
Read a Table

Directions The table shows the number of representatives that seven states had in 1990 and in 2000. Look at the table and answer the questions.

Number of Representatives from Seven States		
State	**Number in 1990**	**Number in 2000**
Arizona	6	8
California	52	53
Colorado	6	7
Mississippi	5	4
New Mexico	3	3
Texas	30	32
Utah	3	3

1 Which state had 32 representatives in 2000? _____

2 Which two states did not gain representatives between 1990 and 2000?

_____

3 How many representatives did Arizona gain between 1990 and 2000?

_____

4 Which state had fewer representatives in 2000 than in 1990?

_____

5 Which state had the most representatives in 2000? _____

_____

Rights and Responsibilities

Directions Read each sentence. Fill in the blank with a word or phrase from the word bank. Use each one only once.

Bill of Rights   religion   vote   ballot   majority rule

1 Adults _____ to elect the President of the United States.

2 When they do this, they mark their choice on a

_____.

3 The person who is chosen by the greatest number of voters becomes

President. This is an example of _____.

4 The part of the Constitution that lists basic rights and freedoms is called

the _____.

5 A _____ is a belief in a god or a set of gods.

Directions Answer the questions.

6 Why is the right to vote also a responsibility?

_____

_____

_____

7 What does the term *minority rights* mean?

_____

_____

_____

Name _____ Date _____

CITIZENSHIP SKILLS

Make a Choice by Voting

Directions Imagine that you are working at an election center. Write how you would describe the voting process to a voter. Write the steps in order.

1 _____

2 _____

3 _____

4 _____

Directions People who vote are proud to be citizens of the United States. Sometimes they wear buttons to show that they are good citizens. Design a button that a voter would be proud to wear. Your button should include the words *I voted*.

Use after reading Chapter 4, Skill Lesson, pages 114–115.

Activity Book ■ **27**

Models of American Citizenship

Directions Match each person with the character trait from his or her biography.

Thomas Jefferson

Harriet Tubman

Helen Keller

Dr. Martin Luther King, Jr.

Joseph Curry

perseverance   fairness   patriotism

civic virtue   courage

Directions Write how these people show their character trait.

Helen Keller _____

_____

Dr. Martin Luther King, Jr. _____

_____

Joseph Curry _____

_____

Harriet Tubman _____

_____

Thomas Jefferson _____

_____

Show Your Pride

Directions Complete the following chart.

Symbol	When I Use It	What I Like Best About It
the flag		
the Pledge of Allegiance		
the national anthem		

Name another symbol of the United States. Tell why this symbol is

important to you. _____

_____

Directions Answer the questions.

1 Which symbol represents the states and the original 13 colonies?

_____

2 Which two symbols honor the flag?

_____

3 Which symbol stands for freedom and is on display in Philadelphia?

_____

What a Responsible Citizen Does

Directions Complete the graphic organizer to show that you understand how to generalize information.

```
┌──────────────┐      ┌──────────────────┐
│    IDEAS     │  →   │  GENERALIZATION  │
└──────────────┘      └──────────────────┘
```

obeys the laws

_____

_____

_____

_____

chooses to vote

_____

_____

_____

_____

_____

_____

_____

_____

_____

_____

_____

_____

_____

_____

_____

_____

Use after reading Chapter 4, pages 100–131.

Name _____ Date _____

4 Test Preparation

Directions Read each question and choose the best answer. Then fill in the circle for the answer you have chosen. Be sure to fill in the circle completely.

1 The part of the federal government that is made up of the Senate and the House of Representatives is—
Ⓐ the Supreme Court.
Ⓑ the city council.
Ⓒ the executive branch.
Ⓓ Congress.

2 The part of the Constitution that names many of the rights and freedoms that belong to all Americans is—
Ⓕ the Bill of Rights.
Ⓖ the Pledge of Allegiance.
Ⓗ the national anthem.
Ⓙ civil rights.

3 In an election, those who do not vote for the winner still keep their rights. This is known as—
Ⓐ majority rule.
Ⓑ minority rights.
Ⓒ common good.
Ⓓ freedom of speech.

4 A slave who helped other slaves escape to freedom was—
Ⓕ Jane Addams.
Ⓖ Dr. Martin Luther King, Jr.
Ⓗ Harriet Tubman.
Ⓙ Helen Keller.

5 Citizens promise to be true to the flag and all that it stands for when they—
Ⓐ fly the flag at half-mast.
Ⓑ say the Pledge of Allegiance.
Ⓒ fly the flag over Fort McHenry.
Ⓓ sing the national anthem.

© Harcourt

Use after reading Chapter 4, pages 100–131.

What Do You See?

Directions Label the landforms, body of water, plants, and animals in the picture. Write a paragraph describing the place.

_____

_____

_____

_____

_____

Name _____ Date _____

MAP AND GLOBE SKILLS
Read a Landform Map

Directions Study this landform map. Then fill in the correct letter to complete each statement.

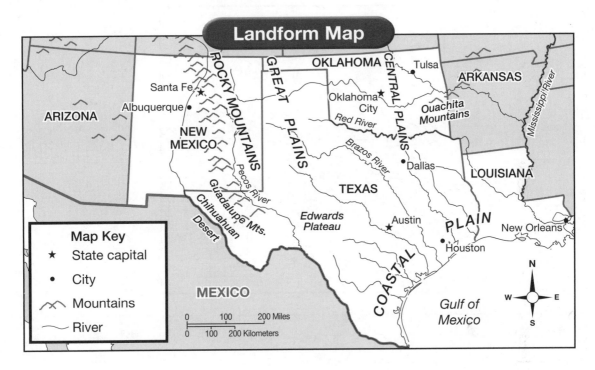

Landform Map

ARIZONA

Santa Fe ★
Albuquerque •
NEW MEXICO

ROCKY MOUNTAINS

GREAT PLAINS

OKLAHOMA
Tulsa •
Oklahoma City ★
Red River

CENTRAL PLAINS

ARKANSAS
Ouachita Mountains

Mississippi River

Pecos River

Guadalupe Mts.

Chihuahuan Desert

Brazos River

Dallas •
TEXAS

Edwards Plateau

Austin ★

Houston •

COASTAL PLAIN

LOUISIANA

New Orleans •

Map Key
★ State capital
• City
⌃⌃ Mountains
〜 River

MEXICO

Gulf of Mexico

0   100   200 Miles
0   100   200 Kilometers

N W E S

---

1 The river that forms part of the border between Texas and Oklahoma is the—
Ⓐ Mississippi River.
Ⓑ Pecos River.
Ⓒ Red River.
Ⓓ Brazos River.

2 Mountains are NOT found in—
Ⓕ Texas.
Ⓖ Louisiana.
Ⓗ Oklahoma.
Ⓙ New Mexico.

3 A city that is located on the Coastal Plain is—
Ⓐ Dallas, Texas.
Ⓑ Houston, Texas.
Ⓒ Santa Fe, New Mexico.
Ⓓ Tulsa, Oklahoma.

4 Edwards Plateau is found in—
Ⓕ central Texas.
Ⓖ southern Louisiana.
Ⓗ eastern Arkansas.
Ⓙ western New Mexico.

© Harcourt

Use after reading Chapter 5, Skill Lesson, pages 152–153.

Changes to the Land

Directions List four features that humans have added to the land in the picture. Give at least one reason why people may have made each change.

Human Features	Reasons for Changes
1 _____	_____
2 _____	_____
3 _____	_____
4 _____	_____

5 Tell how the human features in the picture are similar to and different from the human features in your own community.

_____

_____

_____

© Harcourt

Name _____   Date _____

CHART AND GRAPH SKILLS
Predict a Likely Outcome

Directions Study the chart below. Use what you know about predicting a likely outcome to answer the questions.

Number of Students and Teachers in Fairview Schools		
Year	Teachers	Students
1996	23	612
1998	29	791
2000	51	1,381
2002	56	1,512
2004	not yet determined	not yet determined

1. How did the number of students and teachers in Fairview schools change from 1996 to 2002? _____

2. In which two years did Fairview schools have the highest numbers of teachers? _____

3. What do you predict will happen to the number of students in Fairview schools in 2004? Why? _____

_____

4. If the number of students continues to grow, would you expect the number of teachers to grow as well? Why? _____

_____

_____

Name _____ Date _____

Survival Skills

Directions Imagine that settlers have just arrived to build a community in the place shown in the picture. Think about what the people will do to survive in the area. Then answer the questions.

1 How might the people use the resources shown here to build shelter?

_____

2 How will the settlers stay warm in winter? _____

_____

3 What will the settlers do for food? _____

_____

4 Besides homes, what other things might the settlers build later on to

meet the needs of the community? _____

_____

Use after reading Chapter 5, Lesson 3, pages 160–165.

© Harcourt

Name _____   Date _____

MAP AND GLOBE SKILLS
Find Intermediate Directions

Directions Follow the directions to find locations on the map. Each time you reach a location, write down the name of the item from the shopping list that you could buy there. Then start from that place and follow the next set of directions.

Shopping List

in-line skates
board game
apples
radio
cat food
book

Hardware Store ■	■ Video Store	Toy Store ■
Pet Supply Store ■	Sporting Goods Store ■	Electronics Store ■
Community Park ■	Bookstore ■	■ Farmer's Market

N
NW   NE
W ←◈→ E
SW   SE
S

1 Start at Community Park. Walk northeast for 2 blocks. What item could you buy at this location? _____

2 Now walk south for 1 block. What item could you buy at this

location? _____

3 Next go southwest for 1 block. What item could you buy at this

location? _____

4 Then go northwest for 1 block. What item could you buy at this

location? _____

5 Now travel east for 1 block. What item could you buy at this location?

_____

6 Finally go southeast for 1 block. What item could you buy at this

location? _____

Use after reading Chapter 5, Skill Lesson, pages 166–167.   **Activity Book** ▪ **37**

© Harcourt

Make Inferences Based on What You Have Read and What You Know

Directions Complete the graphic organizer to show that you understand how to make inferences.

WHAT THE WRITER IS TELLING ME	WHAT I KNOW	MY INFERENCE
Earth is made up of many kinds of land.		
Physical features include the kind of weather a place has.		
Oceans cover the space between Earth's continents.		
People learn to live in many different environments.		
Natural resources include water, soil, trees, and plants.		

© Harcourt

Use after reading Chapter 5, pages 144–169.

Name _____ Date _____

5 Test Preparation

Directions Read each question and choose the best answer. Then fill in the circle for the answer you have chosen. Be sure to fill in the circle completely.

1 An example of a physical feature is a—
- Ⓐ building.
- Ⓑ ship.
- Ⓒ mountain.
- Ⓓ statue.

2 Places where two routes meet and where many communities have started are—
- Ⓕ crossroads.
- Ⓖ highways.
- Ⓗ plateaus.
- Ⓙ cities.

3 People create mines to—
- Ⓐ harvest crops by hand.
- Ⓑ get the minerals that lie beneath Earth's surface.
- Ⓒ provide food for millions of people.
- Ⓓ grow plants and raise animals.

4 One way people adapt to living in a hot climate is by—
- Ⓕ wearing thick clothing.
- Ⓖ building houses that allow breezes to pass through.
- Ⓗ burning fuels to get energy for heat.
- Ⓙ covering their heads to stay warm.

5 The Panama Canal is an example of a way that people have—
- Ⓐ adapted to their environment.
- Ⓑ used the natural resources of their community.
- Ⓒ changed the physical features of Earth.
- Ⓓ created crossroads for people to come together.

Use after reading Chapter 5, pages 144–169.

Sentence Scramble

Directions Unscramble each group of words to make a complete sentence based on what you have read in the lesson.

1 need you to describe a reference of point a location relative

_____

2 be used a relative both maps can location and globes to determine

_____

3 and its people Earth studies a geographer

_____

4 Doolittle geographer a is William

_____

5 people sometimes the United States to study geographers divide the land and

_____

_____

6 a orbits without crew Earth a satellite is a that spacecraft

_____

7 pictures on take satellites of Earth landforms

_____

8 can be more than included one region a place in

_____

© Harcourt

MAP AND GLOBE SKILLS
Use a Map Grid

Directions Write the letter and number of the grid box where a visitor can find each place. Then give the map a title.

_____

	1	2	3	4	5
A	Fire Dept.	Library — School —	School	Neighborhood	A
B	Mini Mall	Bank	Police Dept.	Oakmont Park	B
C		Park Lane		Silver Lake	Post Office
D	Hospital		Sam's Market		Rico's Cafe

Chestnut Street

Pine Ridge Ave

Birch Road

Oakmont Ave

Maple Drive

Use Your Imagination

Directions Imagine you are a photojournalist. Here's a photo you took of a forest. Write a paragraph about your photo. Give the forest a name. Tell what happened. Explain how it happened. Did it happen quickly or slowly? Was it caused by a natural disaster? What kind? Was it caused by erosion? Then tell how the forest ecosystem has been affected.

_____

_____

_____

_____

_____

_____

_____

Use after reading Chapter 6, Lesson 2, pages 180–185.

© Harcourt

CHART AND GRAPH SKILLS

Compare Bar Graphs

Directions Texas, Oklahoma, and Kansas are three states in "Tornado Alley." Use the bar graphs to answer each question.

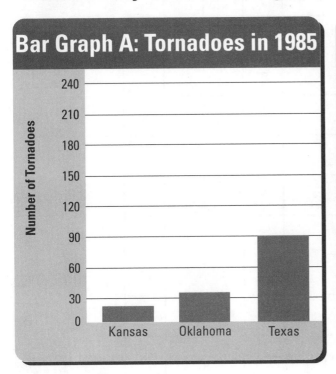

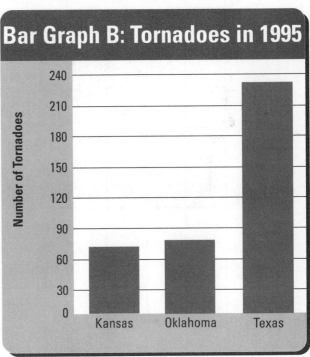

① What natural disaster do these graphs compare? _____

② In Bar Graph A, which state has the most tornadoes? _____

③ In Bar Graph B, which state has the fewest tornadoes? _____

④ Circle about how many tornadoes occurred in Texas and Oklahoma in 1985.

    Over 100

    Under 100

⑤ Were there more tornadoes in these three states in 1985 or in 1995? _____

⑥ Did Kansas have more tornadoes in 1985 or in 1995? _____

⑦ In which year did Texas have fewer tornadoes? _____

© Harcourt

Name _____ Date _____

What's the Word?

Directions Solve the crossword puzzle by writing the words that correctly complete the sentences.

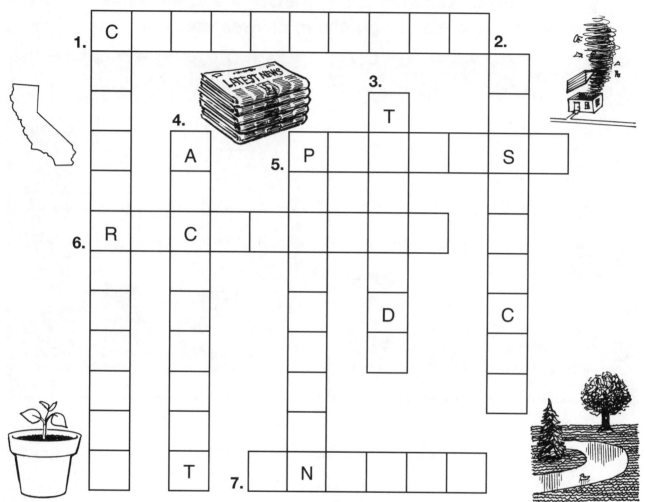

Across

1 Laws in _____ require buildings to be built strong because of earthquakes.

5 Building farms to grow food is a human _____.

6 _____ newspapers, for example, is one way to save trees.

7 Polluted water is _____ to drink.

Down

1 Replanting trees is an example of _____.

2 People use natural _____ such as forests to meet their needs.

3 An underground shelter can protect people in a natural hazard, such as a _____.

4 Some buildings designed by _____ Julia Morgan did not fall during the 1906 San Francisco earthquake.

Use after reading Chapter 6, Lesson 3, pages 188–191.

© Harcourt

Predictions About Geographers

Directions Complete the graphic organizer to show that you understand how to make predictions.

WHAT YOU READ	WHAT YOU KNOW	PREDICTIONS
A geographer is a person who studies Earth and its people. Geographers divide areas of the United States into regions.		

© Harcourt

Name _____ Date _____

6 Test Preparation

Directions Read each question and choose the best answer. Then fill in the circle for the answer you have chosen. Be sure to fill in the circle completely.

1 An area with at least one feature that makes it different from other areas is a—

Ⓐ landform.

Ⓑ region.

Ⓒ relative location.

Ⓓ suburb.

2 In a forest, trees provide all of the following EXCEPT—

Ⓕ food for birds, insects, and other animals.

Ⓖ soil and weather needed for growth.

Ⓗ shade for plants.

Ⓙ shelter for birds, insects, and other animals.

3 Floods, powerful storms, and forest fires are all examples of—

Ⓐ regions.

Ⓑ disasters.

Ⓒ ecosystems.

Ⓓ resources.

4 Suppose that there is an oil spill near where you live. Your water will be—

Ⓕ unsafe to drink.

Ⓖ safe to drink.

Ⓗ clean.

Ⓙ only good for animals to drink.

5 One way to prevent flooding is to—

Ⓐ know what steps to follow during a flood.

Ⓑ construct safe shelters.

Ⓒ stop erosion.

Ⓓ build dams across rivers.

© Harcourt

Use after reading Chapter 6, pages 170–195.

Story Time

Directions Look at the drawings. Then answer the questions.

1 Who are the characters? _____

2 Where did this happen? _____

3 What are the characters doing? _____

Directions Use your imagination to write a few sentences. Tell what you think the characters did next.

_____

_____

_____

_____

_____

_____

READING SKILLS
Tell Fact from Fiction

Directions Read each statement. Then write whether it is fact or fiction. For each statement of fiction, rewrite the sentence on the lines below to make it a fact.

1 Thousands of years ago, Greek and Roman

people told myths. _____

2 Casey Jones jumped on the tracks and held back the engine of the train so it

did not crash. _____

3 Athena was the Greek

goddess of wisdom. _____

4 Daniel Boone used a shovel to

cut down one of the Appalachian Mountains for a pass. _____

5 Casey Jones was on the train that crashed because he took the place

of a sick engineer. _____

6 The Greeks thought Zeus used lightning as a weapon. _____

_____

_____

_____

_____

_____

_____

Who Said It?

Directions Look at the drawings. Then read each quote. Decide which person might have said it. Then write the name on the line.

 **Frederick Douglass**

 **Chief Plenty Coups**

 **Rosa Parks**

 **Jonas Salk**

 **Eleanor Roosevelt**

 **Cesar Chavez**

1 "I was now about twelve years old, and the thought of being a slave for

life began to weigh heavily upon my heart." _____

2 "The ground on which we stand is sacred ground. It is the ground of

our ancestors." _____

3 "My only concern was to get home after a hard day's work."

_____

4 "In the work on polio, I would say that it all went rather smoothly . . . "

_____

5 ". . . Now, I have spent my last night in the White House."

_____

6 "I have met many, many farm workers and friends who love justice and

who are willing to sacrifice for what is right." _____

Where Is It?

Directions Draw a line from each numbered item to the state where it is located.

1 Mount Rushmore   **2** Gateway Arch   **3** Eleanor Roosevelt's house, where the Girls' Leadership Workshop takes place

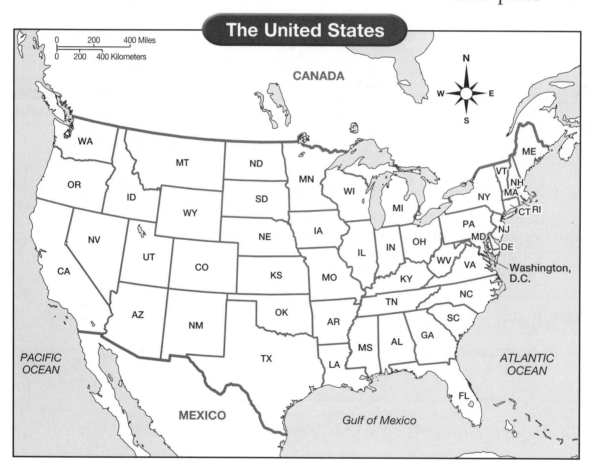

The United States

4 Place where the first Memorial Day was celebrated in 1866   **5** National Statuary Hall   **6** Location of Pilgrim's Thanksgiving celebration in 1621

Name _____ Date _____

Read a Cutaway Diagram

Directions Use the cutaway diagram of a road to answer the questions below.

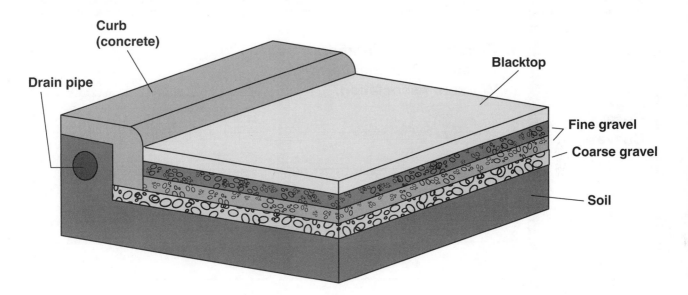

1 What is the bottom layer of the road?

_____

2 What is the layer that you would ride a bike on?

_____

3 Which layer is above the layer of coarse gravel?

_____

4 Which layer is higher than the blacktop layer?

_____

5 Which layer is thickest? _____

6 Which layer is the drain pipe in? _____

© Harcourt

Real American Heroes

Directions Complete the graphic organizer to show that you understand how to summarize information.

HERO	ACTS	SUMMARY
Cesar Chavez	1. Started an organization called the National Farm Workers Association. 2. _____ _____ _____ 3. _____ _____ _____	_____ _____ _____ _____ _____ _____
Eleanor Roosevelt	1. Helped publish a document stating the basic rights of all people. 2. _____ _____ _____ 3. _____ _____ _____	_____ _____ _____ _____ _____ _____

Use after reading Chapter 7, pages 208–239.

Name _____ Date _____

7 Test Preparation

Directions Read each question and choose the best answer. Then fill in the circle for the answer you have chosen. Be sure to fill in the circle completely.

1 The Greeks and Romans used myths to—
Ⓐ explain their religious beliefs.
Ⓑ explain why something in nature is the way it is.
Ⓒ describe brave and clever people.
Ⓓ exaggerate true events.

2 An example of a legend is—
Ⓕ Pecos Bill.
Ⓖ Athena.
Ⓗ Paul Bunyan.
Ⓙ Casey Jones.

3 Jonas Salk developed and tested a vaccine for—
Ⓐ chicken pox.
Ⓑ scarlet fever.
Ⓒ polio.
Ⓓ measles.

4 The memorial that honors United States Presidents and their ideas and leadership is—
Ⓕ Mount Rushmore National Memorial.
Ⓖ the Gateway Arch.
Ⓗ National Statuary Hall.
Ⓙ the Cumberland Gap.

5 The Fourth of July is a national holiday that—
Ⓐ honors Americans who have died in wars.
Ⓑ was established by Abraham Lincoln.
Ⓒ celebrates the birth of the United States.
Ⓓ honors the landing of the Pilgrims.

Coming to the United States

Directions On each line, write a word or words from the box that best fit the description.

Asia and Mexico	immigrant	Madeleine Albright	England
Albert Einstein	Ellis Island	opportunity	

1 the place where many first entered the United States

_____

2 the chance to get a job or have a better way of life

_____

3 where the largest immigrant groups come from today

_____

4 someone who has come to live in a country from another country

_____

5 the country from which the first Europeans came in the 1600s

_____

6 an immigrant whose special skills helped communities around the world in science

_____

7 an immigrant whose special skills helped communities around the world in government

_____

Use after reading Chapter 8, Lesson 1, pages 242–247.

Across the Miles

Directions

1 Imagine you live in Ireland in 1845. Write a postcard to tell a friend in the United States about what is happening in Ireland. Tell your friend that you are coming to the United States. Describe how you feel about the trip.

2 Now imagine you have been in the United States for 2 or 3 months. Write a postcard to a friend in Ireland. Explain what it is like in the United States and how you feel about your new home.

Name _____ Date _____

CITIZENSHIP SKILLS
Make a Thoughtful Decision

Directions On this page is a chart to help you make a thoughtful decision. First, think about a decision you have to make. It might be something such as what you are going to do after school today or what you want to do for your birthday. Fill in the chart. Then make your decision.

1 What do you need to decide? _____

2 Fill in the chart.

Choices	Consequences

3 What decision did you make? _____

_____

4 Why did you make that decision? _____

_____

Name _____ Date _____

Culture Crossword

Directions Complete the crossword puzzle by filling in the answers to the clues below.

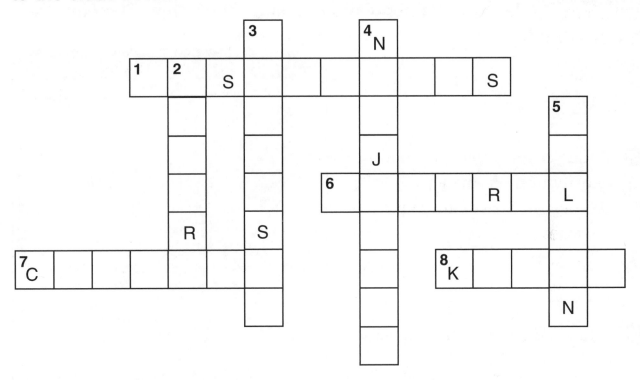

Across

1 A large city on the Pacific coast in southern California.

6 Many of the Spanish-speakers in Los Angeles were born in the United States, but their ancestors were immigrants from Mexico, South America, and _____ America.

7 A large city on the shores of Lake Michigan.

8 In this country, a pickled vegetable treat called *kimchi* is popular.

Down

2 A street in Los Angeles named after the county's first judge, and now a Mexican-style plaza.

3 A city in New Jersey, built near a waterfall, that is one of the oldest cities in the United States.

4 The state where the city of Paterson is located.

5 People of Mexican, Puerto Rican, and Cuban heritage live in this Chicago neighborhood.

Name _____ Date _____

MAP AND GLOBE SKILLS
Use a Population Map

Directions Look at the population density map below. Then answer the questions.

1 What does this map show?

_____

2 Which cities have a population density of more than 100 people per square mile?

_____

_____

3 What is the population density of Susanville?

_____

4 If you wanted to live in a city with only 50–100 people per square mile, where could you live?

_____

5 Describe the population density on the border between California and Oregon.

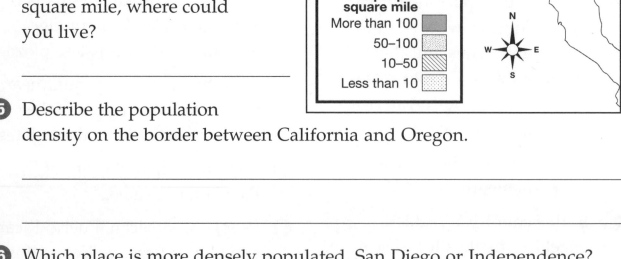

_____

_____

6 Which place is more densely populated, San Diego or Independence?

_____

Use after reading Chapter 8, Skill Lesson, pages 258–259.

Write a Poem

Directions A cinquain is a five-line poem. Here is an example of a cinquain.

Kittens
Silky, soft
Running, leaping, sleeping
Make me smile
Sweet

Follow these steps to write your cinquain. Then draw an illustration of your cinquain.

Line 1: Think of a person, animal, or thing to write about. Write one word to name the subject.

Line 2: Write two words to describe the subject.

Line 3: Write three action words about the subject that end in *-ing*.

Line 4: Write a four or five word phrase that describes the subject (a thought, not a complete sentence).

Line 5: Write one word that means the same thing as the first word or tells what you think of when you read that word.

Name _____ Date _____

Determine Point of View in Pictures

Directions Look at the pictures below. Then answer the questions.

Ⓐ

Ⓑ

1 What is the artist showing about rural Tennessee in picture A?

_____

_____

_____

2 What is the artist showing about urban Tennessee in picture B?

_____

_____

_____

3 What message do you think the artist wants to send in picture A?

_____

_____

4 What message do you think the artist wants to send in picture B?

_____

_____

5 Compare the two pictures. What is both the same and different about the way the artist shows the state of Tennessee? _____

_____

_____

Use after reading Chapter 8, Skill Lesson, pages 266–267.

Name _____ Date _____

Happy Holidays

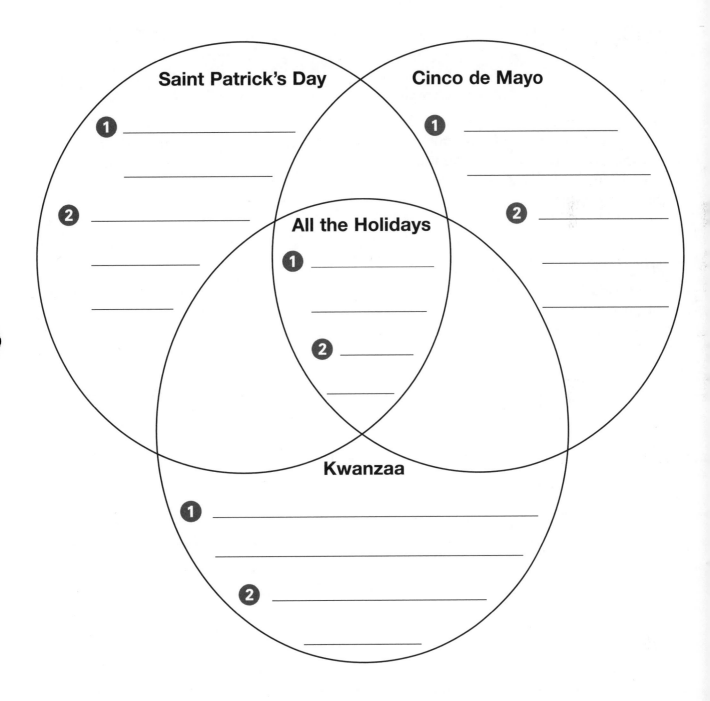

Points of View

Directions Complete the graphic organizer to show that you understand how to determine points of view.

Speaker and Statement	Reason for Statement	Speaker's Point of View	Words Which Show That Point of View
Paul R. Williams: "We must be part of the community in which we live and not apart from it."	To tell how he felt about communities.	People should get along.	"be part of the community"
Author of textbook: American people have a common identity.			

Use after reading Chapter 8, pages 240–275.

8 Test Preparation

Directions Read each question and choose the best answer. Then fill in the circle for the answer you have chosen. Be sure to fill in the circle completely.

1 A former secretary of state who was an immigrant to the United States from Czechoslovakia is—
Ⓐ Pura Belpré.
Ⓑ Madeleine Albright.
Ⓒ Albert Einstein.
Ⓓ Elizabeth Blackwell.

2 A plant disease that killed all the potato crops caused immigrants from what country to come to the United States?
Ⓕ England
Ⓖ Mexico
Ⓗ Ireland
Ⓙ Australia

3 Los Angeles is home to a growing number of immigrants from—
Ⓐ Europe.
Ⓑ Australia.
Ⓒ Africa.
Ⓓ Asia.

4 One kind of drum that comes from Nigeria in Africa is called—
Ⓕ a kalungu.
Ⓖ an icon.
Ⓗ taquería.
Ⓙ kimchi.

5 Cinco de Mayo celebrates—
Ⓐ Mexican independence.
Ⓑ the coming of spring.
Ⓒ a Mexican victory.
Ⓓ traditional Mexican values.

Read About Changes

Directions Read each example of change. Label each example as *Fast Change, Unplanned Change,* or *Unseen Change.*

1 A small community has many businesses that support the nearby farms. There is a drought that goes on for several years. Farmers do not have money to spend. Businesses close and people move away.

_____

2 A new highway is built near a small town. Businesses grow to serve travelers. People move to the town to work for the businesses. The town's size doubles in one year.

_____

3 Joanie get a series of shots to protect her against certain diseases before she begins school. When Joanie's grandmother was young, many of her friends caught measles and whooping cough. Joanie and her friends do not know anyone who has been sick with those diseases.

_____

Directions Choose one of the types of change and write a new example.

Type of change: _____

Example: _____

_____

_____

Name _____ Date _____

READING SKILLS
Identify Cause and Effect

Directions Look at the pictures. If the picture is in column A, write a possible effect in column B. If the picture is in column B, write a possible cause in column A.

<table>
<tr><th>A</th><th>B</th></tr>
</table>

_____
_____
_____
_____

_____
_____
_____

_____
_____
_____
_____

_____
_____
_____
_____

Explore the Past

Directions Think of describing words to put in each box below. Then use those words to help you write a poem about your community's past. You can write a poem with rhyming lines or one with lines that do not rhyme. Write a title for your poem on the top line.

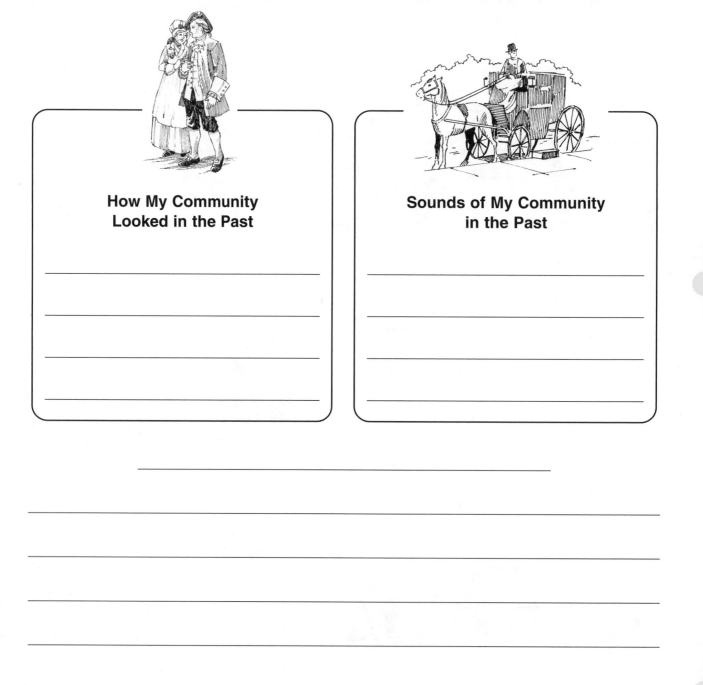

How My Community
Looked in the Past

_____

_____

_____

_____

Sounds of My Community
in the Past

_____

_____

_____

_____

_____

_____

_____

_____

_____

Match the Items

Directions Connect each name with its explanation.

1. Captain John Smith

2. Powhatan

3. England

4. Chesapeake Bay

5. Jamestown

6. Virginia Company

7. Williamsburg

a. Native American leader

b. place the settlers moved to after the first settlement failed

c. first permanent English settlement in North America

d. leader of the group of English settlers

e. group that paid for the settlers' ships and supplies

f. country the settlers came from

g. body of water around which the Native Americans lived

© Harcourt

READING SKILLS
Understand Time Periods

Directions Complete the following activities.

A. List the dates in order from the earliest to the most recent.

1279 B.C.

1901

A.D. 43

1492

_____

_____

_____

_____

2000 B.C.

702 B.C.

1378

1776

_____

_____

_____

_____

B. List the time periods in order from the largest to the smallest.

day

minute

week

year

month

millennium

decade

century

_____

_____

_____

_____

_____

_____

_____

_____

© Harcourt

Ancient Answers

Directions Read the clues. Then write the words in the puzzle spaces.

Across

2 In this form of government, citizens vote for leaders to make decisions.

3 This is a large group of people living in an organized way.

5 Time long past is called this.

6 Early Egyptians built their royal tombs in this shape.

8 Long ago, an Egyptian king was called a _____.

Down

1 In this form of government, citizens make the decisions.

4 Something that has been made for the first time is called an _____.

7 Today we live in _____ times.

Name _____ Date _____

Sequence of Events in the Virginia Colony and Jamestown

Directions Complete the graphic organizer to show that you understand how to sequence events.

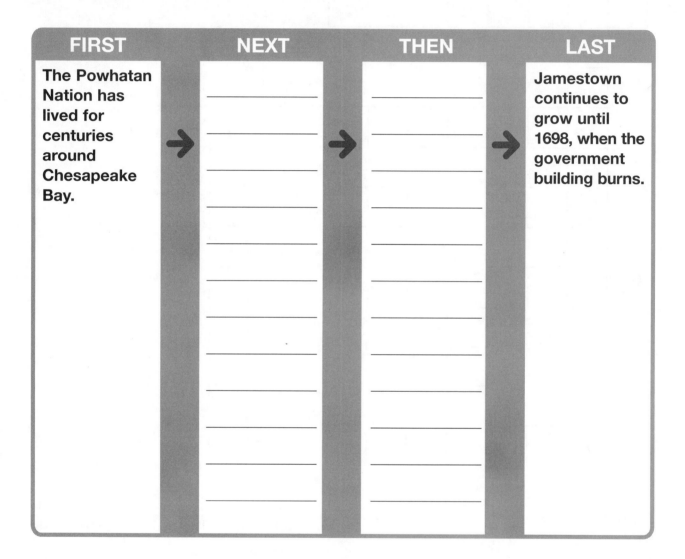

FIRST	NEXT	THEN	LAST
The Powhatan Nation has lived for centuries around Chesapeake Bay.			Jamestown continues to grow until 1698, when the government building burns.

Use after reading Chapter 9, pages 290–323.

Name _____ Date _____

9 Test Preparation

Directions Read each question and choose the best answer. Then fill in the circle for the answer you have chosen. Be sure to fill in the circle completely.

1 Changes in a community may occur over a century, which is—
Ⓐ five years.
Ⓑ ten years.
Ⓒ fifty years.
Ⓓ one hundred years.

2 If a natural disaster such as a hurricane, a flood, or an earthquake happens to a place, it may cause—
Ⓕ planned change.
Ⓖ the population of the place to grow.
Ⓗ great damage and unplanned change.
Ⓙ continuity in the community.

3 Settlers built Jamestown at the mouth of the—
Ⓐ Potomac River.
Ⓑ James River.
Ⓒ Roanoke River.
Ⓓ Susquehanna River.

4 The government of Athens, Greece, became the world's first democracy about—
Ⓕ 2,500 years ago.
Ⓖ 1,500 years ago.
Ⓗ 1,000 years ago.
Ⓙ 500 years ago.

5 For centuries, Mali and other empires were—
Ⓐ democracies.
Ⓑ republics.
Ⓒ important trading centers.
Ⓓ religious centers.

Name _____ Date _____

Native American Groups

Directions Decide which group of people might have made the
following statements. Choose the correct name from the box.
Then write the name of the correct group below each statement.

Sioux Indians	Pueblo Indians	Cahokians

1 "We build our large mounds to honor our dead."

_____

2 "We grow and eat corn, beans, and squash."

_____

3 "We use a travois to move our belongings from place to place."

_____

Directions Choose one of the groups from the box above. Then
write a paragraph from the point of view of a member of that group.
Tell about your life. Describe what you like best about being part of
that group.

_____

_____

_____

_____

Columbus Arrives

Directions The pictures below tell a story. Look at the events shown in the pictures. Then write a paragraph that explains what the pictures show and how the events are related.

_____

_____

_____

_____

_____

Name _____ Date _____

MAP AND GLOBE SKILLS

Follow Routes on a Map

Directions The map shows routes taken by settlers who moved west in the nation's early days. Use the routes shown on the map to answer the questions below.

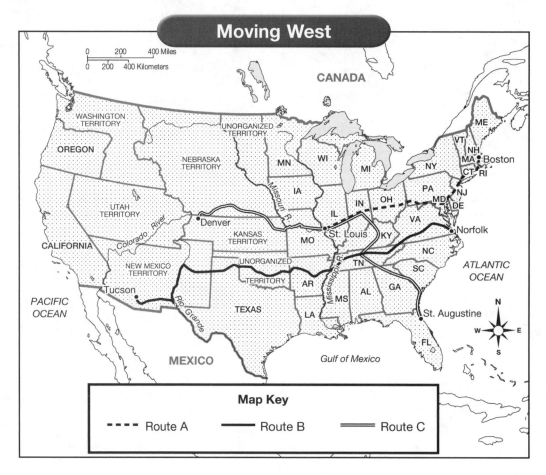

Moving West

CANADA

WASHINGTON TERRITORY

OREGON

UNORGANIZED TERRITORY

NEBRASKA TERRITORY

MN

WI

MI

ME

VT

NH

MA • Boston

NY

CT RI

PA

NJ

MD

DE

IA

UTAH TERRITORY

Denver

Colorado River

KANSAS TERRITORY

MO

IL

IN

OH

St. Louis

KY

VA

Norfolk

CALIFORNIA

NC

ATLANTIC OCEAN

NEW MEXICO TERRITORY

UNORGANIZED TERRITORY

AR

Mississippi R.

TN

SC

Tucson

Rio Grande

TEXAS

LA

MS

AL

GA

St. Augustine

PACIFIC OCEAN

MEXICO

Gulf of Mexico

FL

0   200   400 Miles
0   200   400 Kilometers

N
W   E
S

Map Key

- - - - Route A ——— Route B ═══ Route C

1 Which route goes farthest west on the map? _____

2 Which route goes north and then west? _____

3 Which route on the map is shortest? _____

4 Which route crosses the Rio Grande? _____

5 Of these routes, which would you choose? Why? _____

_____

© Harcourt

Use after reading Chapter 10, Skill Lesson, pages 336–337.

Name _____ Date _____

A Change In Government

Directions Read the following story about the events that happened in America between 1775 and 1789. Fill in the missing words from the story with words from the box. Use each word or group of words only once.

colonies	constitution	Declaration of Independence	revolution
President	fair	battles	

The colonists wanted a change in government. They no longer wanted to be under the rule of England. They began a

_____. The colonists fought against soldiers from England.

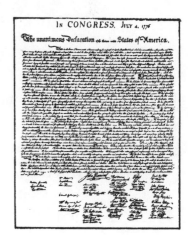

In the _____, representatives of the colonists stated that they wanted to form a new government. Leaders of the

13 _____ accepted this document.

George Washington led the American soldiers in many

_____. Finally, in 1783, the Americans won the war.

The leaders of the new nation wanted laws that

were _____. They came together

to write a _____. After that, the states voted to elect the new country's

first _____. Once again, George Washington became an important leader.

Washington, D.C.

Directions Read the statements below. If the statement is true, write a *T* on the line. If it is false, write an *F* on the line. Cross out the part that is false, and make the statement true.

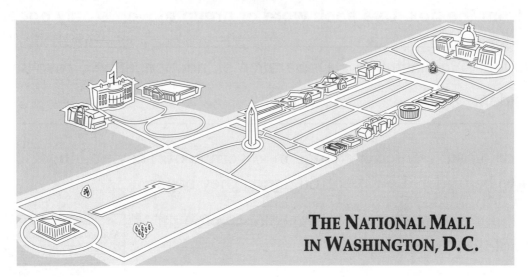

THE NATIONAL MALL
IN WASHINGTON, D.C.

1 _____ Olympia, Washington, is a symbol of our nation's history.

2 _____ In 1791 the Potomac River was in the middle of the United States.

3 _____ The National Mall in Washington, D.C., is a large grassy area that is home to some of the most important buildings and monuments in the United States.

4 _____ L'Enfant was fired because he disagreed with landowners.

5 _____ The capital is the building where our nation's lawmakers meet.

6 _____ Andrew Ellicott and Benjamin Banneker helped plan Washington, D.C.

7 _____ Washington, D.C., lies between Virginia and New York.

8 _____ Thomas Jefferson found a place to build the new city.

Use after reading Chapter 10, Lesson 4, pages 344–349.

Extra! Extra! Read All About It!

Directions Recall what you know about Meriwether Lewis and William Clark, and their contribution to westward expansion. Then write the beginning sentences to the following newspaper story.

The Corps of Discovery Returns Home!

_____

_____

_____

_____

_____

_____

_____

_____

_____

_____

_____

Name _____ Date _____

MAP AND GLOBE SKILLS
Compare History Maps

Directions Study the two maps of Boston, Massachusetts. Then answer the questions that follow.

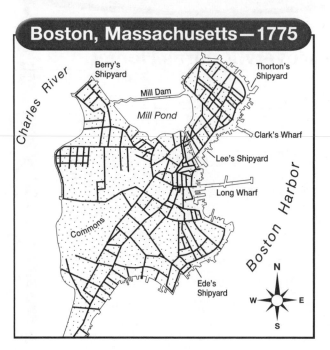

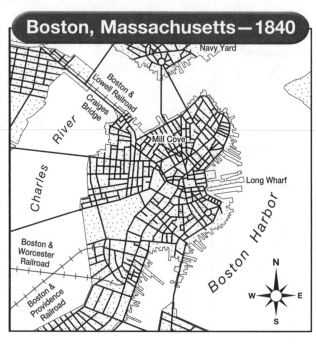

1 What are the dates of the maps? _____

2 What human-made feature is shown on both maps? _____

3 Which map shows railroads? _____

4 What are the names of the railroads? _____

_____

5 Compare the two maps. What generalizations can you make?

_____

_____

_____

Use after reading Chapter 10, Skill Lesson, pages 356–357.

Name _____ Date _____

It's Time for Technology

Directions Look at each picture below. Then answer the questions.

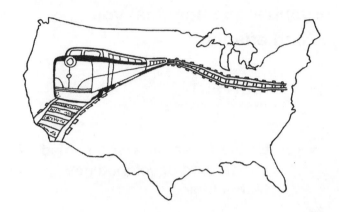

1 What type of railroad is this? How did it change our country?

_____

_____

_____

_____

2 What is this invention? How did it change our country?

_____

_____

_____

_____

3 What is this person doing? How has this changed our country?

_____

_____

_____

_____

Name _____ Date _____

Early People's Changes and Growth

Directions Complete the graphic organizer to show that you understand how to identify the causes and effects.

| CAUSE | | EFFECT |

Early people learned to survive by becoming farmers.

Native Americans who settled and farmed developed new technologies.

_____

_____

The city of Cahokia was home to more than 10,000 people.

Native Americans living in Cahokia built large mounds to honor their dead leaders.

_____

_____

Use after reading Chapter 10, pages 324–363.

© Harcourt

Name _____   Date _____

10 Test Preparation

Directions Read each question and choose the best answer. Then fill in the circle for the answer you have chosen. Be sure to fill in the circle completely.

1 In his travels, Columbus first reached what we now call—
Ⓐ the Indies.
Ⓑ part of Asia.
Ⓒ Corpus Christi, Texas.
Ⓓ the Americas.

2 What document told everyone that the thirteen colonies no longer belonged to England and were now states in the new nation of the United States?
Ⓕ the Bill of Rights
Ⓖ the Declaration of Independence
Ⓗ the Constitution
Ⓙ the Revolutionary War

3 The capital city was built along the Potomac River between the states of—
Ⓐ Florida and Georgia.
Ⓑ Texas and Oklahoma.
Ⓒ Virginia and Maryland.
Ⓓ Ohio and Pennsylvania.

4 The explorations of Lewis and Clark—
Ⓕ led to the formation of English colonies.
Ⓖ caused the Civil War.
Ⓗ helped open the western lands to American settlement.
Ⓙ led to the first maps of the United States.

5 The telegraph was invented by—
Ⓐ Neil Armstrong.
Ⓑ Samuel Morse.
Ⓒ Yuri Gagarin.
Ⓓ Alexander Graham Bell.

Use after reading Chapter 10, pages 324–363.

Name _____   Date _____

Complete the Story

Directions Read the paragraphs below.
Fill in each blank with the correct
word or words from this list.

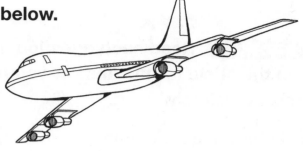

Several companies are

_____ of
airplanes. To build the planes, they need many of
the same things that Henry Ford needed to make
his cars.

| assembly line |
| capital resources |
| human resources |
| producers |
| raw materials |

Constructing factories in which to build planes
is very expensive. Companies need

_____ to buy the equipment
necessary to build the planes.

Steel, aluminum, and other materials used to make the planes are called

_____. Natural resources are also used.

The workers who build the planes are important to the companies that

build and sell planes. These people, called _____,
have the skills to put together the planes. Their skills make the planes well
built and safe to fly.

Inside huge factory buildings the workers build the planes on an

_____. Cars are not the only products made by
having each worker add a part. Planes are built this way, too. As with cars,
building planes this way makes them less expensive.

MAP AND GLOBE SKILLS

Read a Product Map

Directions Use this map to answer the questions below.

1 Are you more likely to find cattle ranches in the north or the south of California?

_____

2 Which two types of crops are grown the most around Monterey Bay?

_____

3 What three kinds of agricultural products are raised near the border between California and Mexico?

_____

4 Which product is grown in more places in California, cotton or hay?

_____

5 If you were a rice farmer, which city would you live closest to?

_____

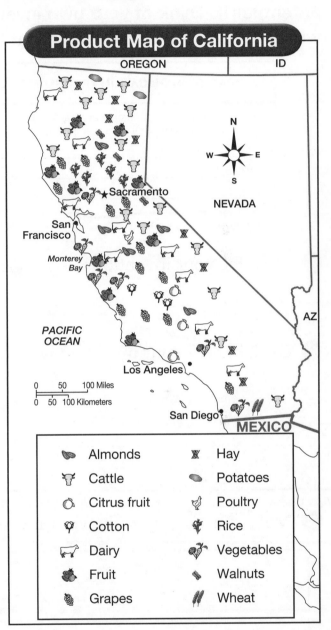

Product Map of California

OREGON   ID

NEVADA

AZ

PACIFIC OCEAN

Sacramento ★

San Francisco •

Monterey Bay

Los Angeles •

San Diego •

MEXICO

0   50   100 Miles
0   50   100 Kilometers

🌰 Almonds	Ⓧ	Hay
🐂 Cattle	🥔	Potatoes
🍊 Citrus fruit	🐔	Poultry
🌱 Cotton	🌾	Rice
🐄 Dairy	🌿	Vegetables
🍓 Fruit	🌾	Walnuts
🍇 Grapes	🌾	Wheat

© Harcourt

What's Your Idea?

Directions When Jeanie Low invented her step stool, she got a patent for it. Think of your own invention. Then fill out the form you would need to send to get a patent for it.

PATENT APPLICATION TRANSMITTAL LETTER	Docket Number (Optional)

To the Commissioner of Patents and Trademarks:
Transmitted herewith for filing under 35 U.S.C. 111 and 37 CFR 1.53 is the patent application of

_____

entitled _____

_____

Enclosed are:

1 Describe your invention. _____

_____

2 Explain how your invention works. _____

_____

_____

_____

3 Make drawings to show your invention.

Advertise It!

Directions Look at the advertisement for Billy's Bagels. Then think of a product you would like to write an advertisement for. It could be a toy, a food, or something else. Then follow the directions to create your ad.

Headline Write a headline for your product.

Picture Draw a picture of your product. The drawing should make the product look like something readers would want to buy.

Description Explain what your product is and why readers should buy it.

Billy's Bagels ← Headline

← Picture

Right out of the oven!

Get your fresh, delicious bagels at Billy's Bagels. Your first bagel is FREE! → Description

READING SKILLS
Tell Fact from Opinion

Directions The statements below are based on the newspaper advertisement. Tell whether each is a fact or an opinion and why you think so.

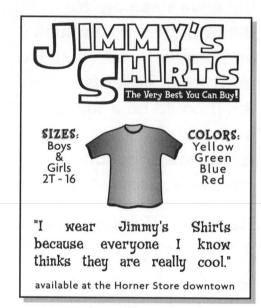

1 Jimmy's shirts come in blue, red, green, and yellow.

_____

_____

_____

2 You can buy Jimmy's shirts at the Horner Store downtown.

_____

_____

3 These are the very best shirts you can buy! _____

_____

4 They come in sizes 2T to 16 for boys and girls.

_____

_____

5 "I wear Jimmy's shirts because they are really cool."

_____

_____

Use after reading Chapter 11, Skill Lesson, pages 400–401.

Let's Party!

Directions You have $50 to spend on your birthday party. You plan to have seven people at the party. Decide how you will spend your money, and fill in the blanks to show how many of the items you will buy. Then explain why you chose those items.

Decorations

Balloons, $2 each _____

Happy Birthday posters, $5 each _____

Party Favors

Goody bag for each guest, with a pen and a game, $3 each _____

Fancy pencil for each guest, $1 each _____

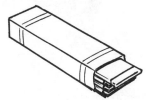

Pack of gum for each guest, 75¢ each _____

Snacks

Popcorn, $3 _____

Peanuts, $2 _____

Pretzels, $2 _____

Drinks

Fruit Juice, $3 per gallon _____

Milk, $4 per gallon _____

Food

Large pizza, $15 _____

Grilled-cheese sandwiches, $4 each _____

What is the total cost of what you want to buy? _____

Why did you choose those items? _____

_____

Where Is It From?

Directions On this page are some products you may have in your home. For each one you find, look at the package or the tag. See if you can find out where the item was made. You may want to ask an adult if you are not sure. Write the name of the country on the line below each picture.

Videotape
or DVD from:

_____

Food
from: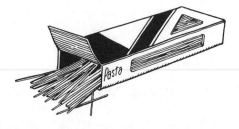

_____

Sneakers
from:

_____

Hat
from:

_____

Shirt
from:

_____

Toy
from:

_____

Use after reading Chapter 11, Lesson 5, pages 406–411.

© Harcourt

Name _____   Date _____

MAP AND GLOBE SKILLS
Use Latitude and Longitude

Directions Use the map to answer the questions below.

1 What Texas city is located at 32°N latitude?

_____

2 What four Texas cities are between 98°W longitude and 96°W longitude?

_____

_____

3 What latitude is Corpus Christi closest to?

_____

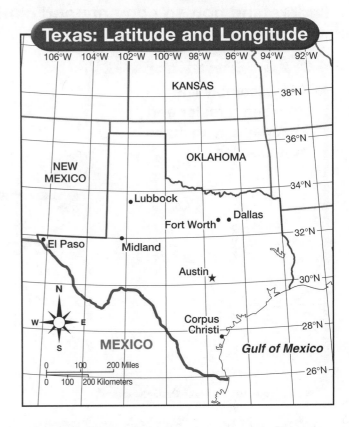

Texas: Latitude and Longitude

4 Which Texas city is closest to 30°N latitude?

_____

5 What Texas city is between 32°N and 34°N latitude and between 102°W

and 100°W longitude? _____

© Harcourt

Compare and Contrast Inventions

Directions Complete the graphic organizer to show that you understand how to compare and contrast information.

Assembly Line

The assembly line provided a faster and cheaper way to make automobiles.

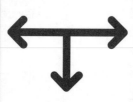

Daguerreotype

Before the daguerreotype introduced photography, all pictures were drawn or painted by artists.

What These Inventions Have in Common

_____

_____

_____

_____

_____

_____

Use after reading Chapter 11, pages 376–415.

© Harcourt

11

Name _____ Date _____

Test Preparation

Directions Read each question and choose the best answer. Then fill in the circle for the answer you have chosen. Be sure to fill in the circle completely.

1 The person who first used an assembly line was—
- Ⓐ Louis Daguerre.
- Ⓑ Henry Ford.
- Ⓒ Cyrus McCormick.
- Ⓓ Granville T. Woods.

2 The machine that made it easier and quicker to harvest grain was—
- Ⓕ the reaper.
- Ⓖ the automobile.
- Ⓗ steam power.
- Ⓙ Torque Control System.

3 The amount of money it takes to run a business is called—
- Ⓐ profit.
- Ⓑ wage.
- Ⓒ overhead.
- Ⓓ competition.

4 If there is a low demand for a product and a high supply of it, the price will usually be—
- Ⓕ very high.
- Ⓖ low.
- Ⓗ very low.
- Ⓙ fair.

5 The dependence of countries on one another for goods and services is known as—
- Ⓐ independence.
- Ⓑ interdependence.
- Ⓒ technology.
- Ⓓ exporting.

© Harcourt

It's Your Choice

(Directions) Imagine you earn $100 a month. Below are some of the ways you could spend your money. Choose what you would like to buy, and write the prices in the *Total* column. You may also want to save some money. Make sure that the cost of items you choose do not total more than $100.

Item	Cost	Total
Bike	$ 80	
Book	$ 10	
Toy	$ 7	
Game	$ 20	
Amusement park ticket	$ 35	
Movie and popcorn	$ 10	
Pants	$ 25	
Shoes	$ 30	
Gift for a friend	$ 10	
Savings	$ 15	
	Total	

Use after reading Chapter 12, Lesson 1, pages 418–421.

CHART AND GRAPH SKILLS
Read a Flow Chart

Directions Use the information below to create a flow chart.
Number and label the steps in the order in which they should be
done. Also add arrows. The first step has been done for you.

1 Prepare _____

soil.

_____

_____

_____

_____

_____

_____

_____

Here are the steps needed to plant carrot seeds so they grow into
delicious vegetables. First, prepare the garden soil. It should be crumbly.
Next, scatter the seeds on the soil. Place about a half-inch of soil on top
of the seeds. When you see the tiny green shoots of the carrots in about a
week, thin the plants. Pull up the weakest plants so that there is one carrot
plant about every two inches. While the plants grow, make sure they are
watered often. Finally, harvest the carrots in about two months.

You Are the Banker!

Directions Create a brochure that describes the services your bank offers. Read about each part of the brochure. Then write sentences that explain each part.

Name of the Bank: Make up a name for your bank.

Checking: Explain how a checking account works.

Savings: Explain how a savings account works.

The Bank for You!
We offer these services.

Checking: _____

_____

_____

_____

_____

Savings: _____

_____

_____

_____

_____

_____

Use after reading Chapter 12, Lesson 2, pages 424–427.

Name _____ Date _____

CHART AND GRAPH SKILLS
Use a Line Graph

Directions Use the stock information for Clare's Clothing Company to make a line graph. Then answer the questions below.

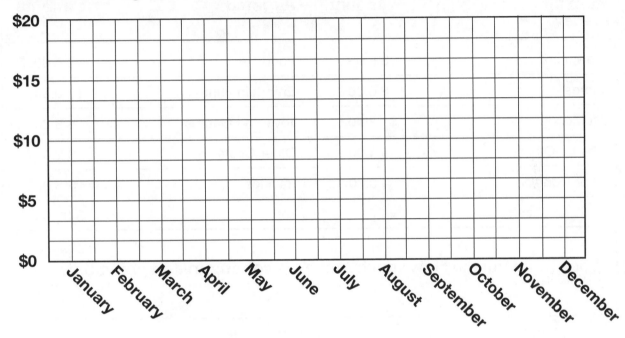

Last year, you bought one share of stock in Clare's Clothing Company. Here is the price of the share of stock every month since you bought the stock.

Clare's Clothing Company

January $5	February $7	March $10
April $7	May $10	June $12
July $15	August $10	September $12
October $15	November $17	December $19

1 Did the price of the stock in Clare's Clothing Company go up or down from October to December? _____

2 When was the stock price at its lowest? _____

3 Was stock in Clare's Clothing Company a good investment? Explain.

_____

© Harcourt

Make a Budget

Directions This is how much Bailey earned and spent in one week. Use the information to answer the questions below.

Incoming Money	Amount	Outgoing Money	Amount
Allowance	$ 5.00	Food	$ 5.00
Chores	$ 6.00	Entertainment	$ 10.00
Gift Money	$ 12.00	Toys and Games	$ 5.00
Jobs for Others	$ 4.00	Other Costs	$ 2.00
Other Income	$ 0.00	Savings	$ 5.00
Total	$ 27.00	Total	$ 27.00

1 Look at the totals. How much money is coming in and going out?

_____

2 Bailey would like to buy a new bicycle. The bicycle she wants costs $120. How can she use the information in the chart to reach her goal?

_____

_____

_____

_____

3 How can Bailey reach her goal? _____

_____

Use after reading Chapter 12, Lesson 3, pages 430–433.

© Harcourt

Name _____ Date _____

Make an Economic Choice

Directions Use the information on this page to help you make an economic choice.

Restaurant Meal

Meal at Home

You are hungry for lunch. You have the choice of going out to a restaurant to eat and spending your money, or fixing a meal at home and saving your money. Use the steps below to make your choice.

Step 1. Think about the trade-offs.
What do you have to give up to have the restaurant meal?

_____

_____

What do you have to give up to have the meal at home?

_____

_____

Step 2. Think about the opportunity costs.
What is the opportunity cost of the restaurant meal?

_____

_____

What is the opportunity cost of the meal at home?

_____

_____

Step 3. Make a Decision.
What will you decide? Why will you make this decision?

_____

_____

People Who Share

Directions Fill in each blank with the correct word from the lesson. Then find and circle the word in the puzzle. The words may go up and down, across, or on a diagonal.

Y	N	E	S	V	O	O	P
I	D	B	C	R	O	S	S
L	A	O	T	W	D	N	P
C	A	R	N	E	G	I	E
E	B	D	R	A	Y	C	A
A	T	E	I	H	T	R	C
B	A	R	T	O	N	E	E
S	P	S	K	I	L	L	S

1 Andrew _____, the richest man in the world in 1901, spent his fortune for the public good.

2 In the United States, the Red Crescent is called the Red _____.

3 _____ Corps volunteers work in communities around the world.

4 When someone gives away money to help those who have less, he or she _____ it.

5 Some people enjoy sharing their money, time, and _____ with others.

6 Some doctors work without pay in a group called Doctors Without

_____.

7 Clara _____ started the American Red Cross.

Use after reading Chapter 12, Lesson 4, pages 436–441.

Name _____ Date _____

Tell Fact From Opinion About Earning and Saving Money

Directions Complete this graphic organizer to show that you understand how to tell facts from opinions.

TOPIC	FACT	OPINION
Earning Money	Today one of every three workers in the United States earns an income from a service job.	_____ _____ _____ _____
Saving Money	_____ _____ _____	_____ _____ _____

Name _____ Date _____

Test Preparation

Directions Read each question and choose the best answer. Then fill in the circle for the answer you have chosen. Be sure to fill in the circle completely.

1 A clerk in a clothing store selling shirts and jeans earns—
Ⓐ an investment.
Ⓑ an income.
Ⓒ interest.
Ⓓ a budget.

2 Interest is the money—
Ⓕ people set aside for an emergency.
Ⓖ people receive when an investment grows in value.
Ⓗ people are paid for working.
Ⓙ a bank pays a person for keeping his or her money in the bank.

3 To reach their goal for purchasing items, people should—
Ⓐ make an investment.
Ⓑ gather information.
Ⓒ make a budget.
Ⓓ have a larger income.

4 The famous American who founded the American Red Cross was—
Ⓕ Andrew Carnegie.
Ⓖ Jane Addams.
Ⓗ Clara Barton.
Ⓙ Harriet Tubman.

5 A volunteer organization in which citizens of the United States share their skills to help people around the world is—
Ⓐ the Peace Corps.
Ⓑ the Chow Hound.
Ⓒ Second Harvest.
Ⓓ Meals on Wheels.

Use after reading Chapter 12, pages 416–443.